THE BOOK OF ILLUSIONS

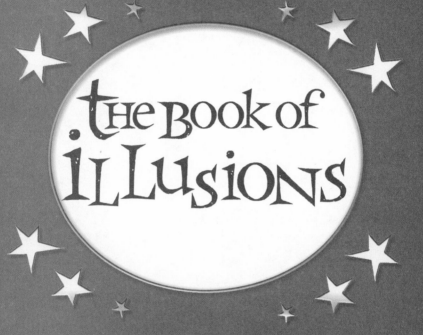

THE BOOK OF iLLUSIONS

by Tom Mason and Dan Danko
with Jeff Fredriksen, Professional Magician

Scholastic Inc.
New York • Toronto • London • Auckland • Sydney
Mexico City • New Delhi • Hong Kong • Buenos Aires

ISBN 0-439-32702-4

Copyright © 2001 by Scholastic Inc.

Design by Mark Neston
Illustrations by Daniel Aycock

12 11 10 9 8 7 6   2 3 4 5 6/0

Printed in the U.S.A.

First Scholastic printing, October 2001

tABLe of CoNteNts

the magic of ILLUSIONS

Q uick question: What looks real but really isn't? A toupee is a good guess. But this isn't Toupee University. It's Magic University! Besides, a toupee never really *looks* real, does it?

In the big, cool world of magic, what *looks* real but really isn't is...an *illusion*.

Magicians are experts at the art of illusion. They can have you seeing one thing but believing something else. To put it another way: Seeing isn't always believing.

Pulling a rabbit out of a hat and sawing someone in half are classic examples of illusions. (Sorry, you won't be learning the rabbit-from-a-hat trick, but, surprise, you will learn the sawing-in-half one!)

Harry Houdini used to walk through a brick wall. David Copperfield once walked through an even bigger one: the Great Wall of China! Magicians love to make the audience believe that solid objects might not be as solid as they seem to be. Magicians fool our senses: We know what we saw, what we heard, and what we felt. It was all so real.

Or was it? That's the beauty of an illusion. You saw it. You believe it. But what did you really see?

Now it's your turn to make that same kind of magic and to leave your audience wondering just what the heck really happened. You'll learn how to push a pencil through a quarter, how to melt a penny through someone's hand, and how to pretend to chop off your own finger. (Don't worry: You won't draw blood; in fact, you won't even be touching your finger at all!)

By using the magic tricks from your ILLUSIONS KIT and some everyday stuff from around the house like quarters, newspapers, and drinking glasses, you'll join the magicians of history by inviting your audience to ask one simple question: What is real and what is illusion?

And then, after they've asked, don't tell 'em! You went to Magic University and they didn't. You know the secret and they don't.

That's the way it should be. That's the way to keep the magic of illusions!

—Tom Mason and Dan Danko

THE tRICKS

PENCIL PUSHING

assignment: Push three pencils through three coins!

pushing pencils

Great gimmicks make great illusions! The Magic Three-hole Coin Box has a hidden tray that slides the coins out of the pencils' way and lets the pencils pass through!

magic must-haves: Magic trunk

homemade magic: Three quarters, three (sharpened) pencils, a piece of paper, a pair of scissors

from your illusions kit: Magic Three-hole Coin Box

backstage

There's lots to do before you start, so sit up straight and pay attention—like you would in algebra class if you really liked math. The Three-hole Coin Box comes with its own special key: It's that flat plastic thing with a little point on the end—you should find it when you lift the lid of the Coin Box. The key locks and unlocks a hidden tray at the bottom of the box. To release the tray, push the pointed end of the key into the small, round piece of the hinge that sticks out from the top left side of the Coin Box. Tilt the Coin Box slightly downward and to the left; the tray should slide right out. Then slide the tray back to its starting position. Once the tray is back, you can lock it by pushing in the little knob that sticks out of the hinge on the top right side of the Coin Box.

Next, get the scissors, and cut the piece of paper so that it's about 1 1/4 inches wide and 6 inches long. It should be wide enough to fit inside the Coin Box and long enough to stick out on both sides by at least three fourths of a inch. The length is important because when you get around to sliding out the hidden tray, you want the paper to keep the tray hidden from the audience. The paper will serve as evidence, but we'll get to that later!

To start, hide the key in your pocket or somewhere else handy, but keep the piece of paper on the magic trunk, next to the three pencils and the three quarters.

SHOW time!

"Pushing a solid object through another solid object: Science says it's impossible, but magic lets me do it anyway."

STEP 1: Show the Three-hole Coin Box to the audience. The hidden tray should be unlocked but still hidden. Open the lid, and let the audience watch as you place the three quarters inside, one at a time.

"I've got three quarters that are about as solid as you can get."

STEP 2: Place the piece of paper on top of the coins, like you were covering them with a blanket— a tiny paper blanket. Close the lid of the Coin Box. The paper should overhang both sides of the box evenly.

"And one piece of paper, which is also solid."

STEP 3: Turn the case slightly downward and to the left, and release the hidden tray. It should slide out easily and be hidden by the overhanging paper. Pick up one of the pencils with your free hand.

"The key to this trick is that I have to use my magician's breath. That's why it's important for magicians to brush their teeth after every meal."

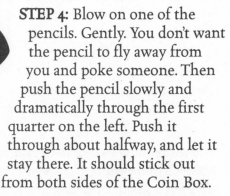

STEP 4: Blow on one of the pencils. Gently. You don't want the pencil to fly away from you and poke someone. Then push the pencil slowly and dramatically through the first quarter on the left. Push it through about halfway, and let it stay there. It should stick out from both sides of the Coin Box.

"This transfers the magic from me directly to the pencils..."

STEP 5: Repeat step 4 with the second pencil and the second quarter.

"...so they can push their way..."

STEP 6: And repeat step 4 one more time with the last pencil and the third quarter. All three pencils should be sticking out of both sides of the Coin Box.

"...through the solid quarters."

STEP 7: Reach around the front of the Coin Box with your right hand, and slowly pull the pencils out, one at a time—like King Arthur pulling the sword out of the stone (except that no wrinkled old wizard's going to crown you king!). As you pull out the last pencil, slide the tray closed with any finger on your left hand that's comfortable for you.

"Let's take a look at the evidence."

STEP 8: Open the lid of the Coin Box, and hold up the paper to show the holes. One at a time, dump the coins on the trunk so the audience can see them.

> **Trick Tip:** When you're feeling confident about this trick, ask one of the audience members to step up and pull the pencils out.

"There are lots of liars in the world, but paper always tells the truth. The magic pencils went right through the quarters."

STEP 9: As the audience leans forward to study the coins, casually relock the tray. This can be done by pushing in the small rod that sticks out of the hinge on the far right side.

"But the quarters are still in perfect shape. Maybe some of the pencil's magic rubbed off on them!"

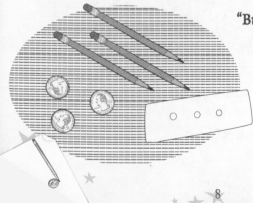

STEP 10: Now, leave the lid of the Coin Box open, and place it on the trunk. Let anybody from the audience pick up the Coin Box and look at it for as long as they want; only you have the key that opens the slide, so your secret is safe!

HOMEWORK: Slide the tray out and back with one smooth move so the audience won't be able to see what you're doing.

COINS THAT VANISH

Most people make coins disappear by spending them. But magicians have been doing magic with coins for hundreds of years. In fact, the very first magic trick book, *The Discoverie of Witchcraft* by Reginald Scott (1584), has a few great coin tricks. In one of them, a coin is made to vanish from one hand and reappear in the other. This has become a magic classic and is known by magicians as the *Sympathetic Coins*. In his book, Scott explains that coin tricks can be accomplished by using fake coins. He tells of a coin that can be made of two coins that have been sliced in half and stuck together back-to-back so that, depending on what side you're looking at, you see a different type of coin. All the magician has to do is to secretly turn the coin over, and the audience will think that the first coin has left the magician's hand and another coin has taken its place!

WHOPPER CHOPPER #2

Lesson: Make the audience believe you've chopped off your finger!

Slice and dice

You can't use this Chopper to do any real slicing! The Finger Chopper has a trick "blade" that goes around your finger and not through it. By doing it fast enough, the audience can't tell!

Magic must-haves:

Magic trunk

Homemade magic:

One Band-Aid®

From your illusions kit: Finger Chopper

Backstage

Set up the Chopper on the magic trunk in front of you.

Show time!

"I love scary movies. Monsters in the basement. Crazy zombies. Vampires. And someone's always getting their head cut off. That doesn't really bother me. I know it's just Hollywood special effects."

STEP 1: Pull the Chopper blade all the way out.

"I've got my own special effect right here."

STEP 2: Push the Chopper blade down quickly—fast enough so that the audience doesn't see how the blade is gimmicked, but not so fast that you break the Chopper!

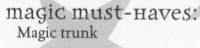

"It's my own portable Chopper! But what could I put in there? My head's way too big. The hole's too small for a banana. A carrot's too big..."

STEP 3: Look at someone in the audience. As you do this, slide your left hand around the front of the Chopper, and pull the blade back up to the starting position with your right hand. This way, no one can see the trick blade as it comes back up.

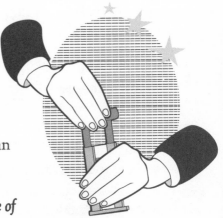

"Perhaps I could borrow one of your fingers?"

STEP 4: Everyone should be nervously laughing by now. If not, it's time to get new friends—'cause that was a pretty funny joke.

"All right. I don't want to risk hurting my audience. You're all potential paying customers someday. I'd better just do this trick myself."

STEP 5: Pull out the Band-Aid, show it to the audience, and place it on the magic trunk.

"Just in case."

STEP 6: Put your finger through the hole in the Chopper. Pause for a second like you're trying to suck up some courage. Take a deep breath. Then push down the Chopper!

"Yes!"

STEP 7: Take a breath so the audience has a chance to enjoy what you've just done. Then, take your finger out of the Chopper, and show it to the audience. If you've done this trick correctly, you should still have all ten digits. If you haven't done it correctly...well, you can still live a perfectly normal life with just nine fingers. (Just kidding!)

> **Trick Tip:** You can have a banana and a carrot on hand to demonstrate that they really are too big for the Chopper.

"Just as good as new."

HOMEWORK: Practice sliding the blade up and down so that the audience can't see how the blade moves around your finger.

MAGIC INVENTOR

Guy Jarrett never performed onstage, but he invented several classic magic illusions for other magicians. One of his marvels was called *The Twenty-one-Person Cabinet*. It appeared in various shows in New York in the 1920s. It was not much bigger than a phone booth, and yet twenty-one people would pile out of it, filling an entire stage. Jarrett claims that no one could figure out its secret and that it even fooled him when he watched it. Now *that's* magic!

exercise: Make a coin disappear and reappear inside four sealed boxes!

pocket money

Bonjour! This trick features a sleight-of-hand motion called the *French Drop*. (And that's not what happens when the Eiffel Tower falls over!) By misdirecting the audience's attention, you'll secretly move a quarter from your hand to your pocket.

homemade magic: One quarter, one marker

extras: One volunteer who doesn't know the trick

from your illusions kit: The Four Nesting Boxes, Magic Box Holder

backstage

The Four Nesting Boxes are so named because the smaller ones are designed to *nest*, or stack, inside the larger ones. Take the four boxes, and split them into two groups—the tops and the bottoms (the bottoms are a little deeper than the tops; that's how you tell them apart). Take all the box bottoms, and fit them inside one another. Do the same with the tops. Place the bottoms in the top part of the Magic Box Holder facing you and the tops facing toward the bottoms in the bottom part of the Box Holder. (Stop! Read through that again, and check the pictures to make sure you really understand it. We'll wait.) With your index finger and thumb, practice sliding the tops and bottoms together to create one box with the three other boxes hidden inside. You'll need to master this move before you start. When

TOPS

BOTTOMS

you're ready, put the Magic Box Holder in your right-hand pocket, arranged just this way. If you don't do it correctly, the tops will become the bottoms and the bottoms will become the tops, and pretty soon we'll sound like a Dr. Seuss book.

show time!

"Every now and then I get some extra money, like this quarter."

STEP 1: Display the quarter to the audience.

"So I don't lose it or get it confused with someone else's quarter, I like to mark it."

STEP 2: Pick a volunteer, give her the marker, and have her mark the quarter with an X. After that's done, hold the quarter between the thumb and index finger of your right hand. Hold your other fingers together.

"And I want to keep my money in a safe place, but you can't really put a quarter in a bank. They'd laugh at me. I could put it in a piggy bank, but then somebody could grab the bank and run off with it."

STEP 3: Now bring your left hand over like it's going to grab the quarter. Watch your finger placement: Your left thumb goes to the back of the quarter, and the fingers go in front.

"But I can't go around carrying my money in my hand all the time."

STEP 4: As your left fingers come in front, the thumb of your right hand releases the quarter. The coin drops easily into the fingers of your right hand!

"I could easily drop my quarter or lose it."

STEP 5: Close your left hand, pretending that it has the quarter, and move it away to your left. The audience is watching your left hand closely. This is the *misdirection*. Now, while they're trying to figure out what's up with your left hand, drop your right hand casually at your side, holding the quarter in your right fingers. *Très bien* (good work)! You've done a French Drop!

"So the only thing I came up with was to hide the money."

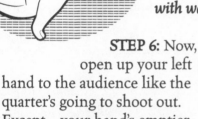

STEP 6: Now, open up your left hand to the audience like the quarter's going to shoot out. Except…your hand's emptier than Death Valley. The quarter is gone!

"And I found the perfect place for it."

STEP 7: Reach into your pocket with your right hand. Do it casually—not like you're digging for gold. As you do this, place the quarter inside the secret nest of boxes. As soon as the quarter's in place, slide the two sets of boxes together, so that one set is on top of the other. Remove all of them as one unit from your pocket. But leave the Box

Holder in your pocket or you'll blow everything!

"It's safer than a bank and better than leaving it in my hand."

Trick Tip: Perform this trick standing behind a table so that the audience can't see the outline of the slide in your pants pocket. Baggy pants help, too! Who knew magic would require special pants?

STEP 8: Remove the top from the outside box. Open the next one. Open the third. Open the fourth to reveal the marked quarter inside.

"Don't you agree?"

HOMEWORK: Practice the French Drop in front of a mirror. It's also important to get really slick at placing the quarter inside the boxes and sealing them up. This should be done in one smooth move. The more you fumble and fiddle, the more the audience will start to suspect!

SPEEDY COINS

At some point in his studies, every magician—including you, one day—learns the *Han Ping Chien Trick*. In addition to being tough to pronounce (which might be the trickiest part of all) Han Ping Chien is a sleight-of-hand move that mysteriously passes a coin from the right to the left hand. Its inventor was a Chinese magician who toured the United States in 1915 and 1916. He taught it to American magicians by revealing "the hand is faster than the eye" secret: The coin is secretly tossed at high speed from one hand to the other!

tHe magic toWeR #4

pROjeCt: Slide a cube through your magic wand!

tHe toWeR tReasuRe

One cube is okay, but two cubes make a great trick. The "cube inside a cube" is a good example of a gimmick. It makes the audience think that one cube is doing the work of two!

magiC must-Haves: Magic wand, magic trunk

fROm yOuR iLLusiOns kit: Six-sided cube, five-sided cube, magic tower

baCkstage

The magic tower is the long rectangular piece of cardboard. Gently push the edges toward each other so that you've got a long tube, and then

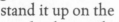

stand it up on the trunk. Then grab the other two funny-looking pieces of cardboard in your kit—those are the five- and six-sided cubes. Put them together by sticking all of the cardboard tabs into the little slits. Take the six-sided cube and place it inside the five-sided cube. Now it looks like you've just got one cube. Turn the five-sided cube upside down, and the six-sided cube will fall out faster than your dad's hair. But keep the two cubes together for the beginning of this trick.

SHOW time!

"You know what I love? Ice cream. But I also love the story of King Arthur and the Knights of the Round Table and the famous wizard, Merlin."

STEP 1: Pick up the tower, and turn it toward the audience to show them that it's empty. Place it back on the magic trunk.

"Someday, I hope to build my own castle and use it as a branch of Magic University, so I can teach magic tricks. And charge tuition. Lots of tuition."

STEP 2: Hold up the five-sided cube (with the six-sided one inside). The empty bottom of the five-sided cube should be facing you. You can show it quickly to the audience, but don't give them time to see that you've got another cube hidden inside! As you hold the cubes, squeeze them just a little so that the two cubes stay together and look like one cube.

"I'm going to have really tall towers in my castle, just like this one here...but I'm not going to have steps inside."

STEP 3: Drop the two-in-one cube down the top of the tower so that the open end of the five-sided cube goes in first.

"A magician doesn't need steps—I'll just float up and down inside the tower."

STEP 4: Grab the tower by the bottom with one hand. Squeeze the tower bottom gently, as if you were holding a kitten, so that you trap the five-sided cube against the inside of the tower, but allow the six-sided cube to fall out onto the magic trunk. Now, lift up the tower. As you lift it, the five-sided cube will remain hidden inside the tower.

STEP 5: Set the tower back down on the magic trunk, next to the six-sided cube. Pick up the six-sided cube, and casually toss it in your hand so the audience sees that it's solid. Toss it to someone in the audience, and have them toss it back. (But don't toss it if you have trouble catching stuff!) Pick up the magic wand with your free hand.

"And, being a magician, I won't have to worry about crashing into anything inside the tower."

STEP 6: Slide the magic wand through the holes in the tower.

"I mean, suppose someone left their gigantic magic wand in the middle of the tower."

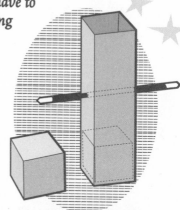

STEP 7: Drop the six-sided cube inside the tower.

"That's no problem at all; a good magician (like myself) will just float right through the wand and down to the bottom of the tower."

STEP 8: The six-sided cube will fall through the tower, but it'll stop when it gets to the wand. Now the trick really gets interesting!

"See?"

STEP 9: Lift up the tower from the middle. This releases the five-sided cube. The audience will think it's the same cube that they saw you drop down the tower in step 7.

Trick Tip: Turn the tower so that one of the sides *without* the holes is facing the audience. That way, they can see both ends of the magic wand, but they can't look through the tower holes and see your cube!

Put the tower away as quickly as possible so no one can see the real six-sided cube inside!

HOMEWORK: Pick up the tower again and again, making sure that you keep the five-sided cube hidden inside as the six-sided cube falls out.

THE HEAVY SHOW

During the Golden Age of Magic in the 1920s, Howard Thurston, known as Thurston the Great, performed his "Wonder Show of the Universe." The equipment he needed for the show took up three whole railroad cars! He had a workshop near his home in Long Island, New York, where his staff of thirty mechanics and cabinet workers built new illusions and props. His favorite contraption was the one that made a woman float in midair. It required twenty-three hundred pounds of equipment, invisible wires, and very special lighting.

the coin press #5

assignment: Magically push a coin through a glass!

pressing coins
This trick is a combination of gimmick and sleight of hand. As you hide one quarter, you release a second quarter from its hiding place in the secret compartment of the disk. It looks like the quarter has mysteriously moved through a solid object!

homemade magic: Two quarters, one handkerchief, one clear plastic drinking glass

from your illusions kit:
The blue disk

backstage
Turn the blue disk upside down. A trapdoor will open up in the disk, like you're in some mad scientist's secret lab. Put one of the quarters inside the trap, and close it up. Take the open end of the glass, and make sure it fits inside the edge of the blue disk or snugly around the outside of the disk.

show time!
"I have a fun trick with this drinking glass that always makes my mom nervous. No, she's not afraid I'll break the glass. She's worried that if I keep practicing my magic tricks, I'll never have time to clean my room."

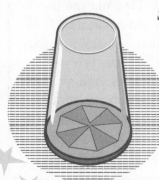

STEP 1: Show the empty glass to the audience. Place it upside down on top of the blue disk, and hold up the second quarter.

"I keep telling her to relax."

STEP 2: Place the second quarter on top of the glass, and cover the glass, the quarter, and the disk with the handkerchief. Hold this setup on your open left palm.

"Even if I weren't practicing my magic, I still wouldn't clean my room!"

STEP 3: Press your index finger down on the second quarter as if you're trying to push it through the glass.

"But, back to the glass. I'm going to push a quarter right through it. With a little magical force ...like so!"

STEP 4: Now, place your right palm over the quarter and the handkerchief. Hold the glass and disk between your two hands, and give it a shake. This releases the quarter from the blue disk. The audience will hear it clink inside the glass.

STEP 5: Pull the handkerchief off the glass with your right hand, picking up the second quarter

Trick Tip: You can use any two duplicate objects—dimes, pennies, two buttons, two very small dogs (well, probably not)—with this trick. Just be sure the object fits into the secret compartment of the blue disk!

with it. After you do that, immediately shove the handkerchief and the quarter into your pocket.

"And the quarter goes right through the glass without breaking it."

HOMEWORK: The key to this trick is hiding the second quarter in step 5. Practice grabbing the quarter with your thumb and hiding it with the handkerchief so the audience won't see it. And be careful not to scrape the quarter across the bottom of the glass!

TOSS ACROSS

Tony Slydini was a master of intricate pocket tricks that require practice in front of a mirror. Born in Argentina, Slydini moved to New York City in 1930 where he performed his miracles with cards and coins. Slydini was best known for crumpling a piece of paper into a ball and making it vanish right before a spectator's eyes. The secret? He was so close to the person's face that he simply tossed the ball over his or her head!

exercise: Make a ball jump from your hand to the inside of an upside-down cup!

Bouncing Balls

Ever wonder how a magician pulls a rabbit out of a hat? So do we. But one thing we do know is how magicians make coins appear behind people's ears or a ball appear under a cup. It's all about *palming*, that is, hiding an object in your hand. By hiding a ball under a cup, then palming a second ball, it creates the illusion the ball has jumped from your hand to the cup.

magic must-haves: Magic trunk

from your iLLusions kit:

One cup, two balls

backstage

Pick a ball, any ball. Drop it in the cup. Shhh! This is our little secret, so make sure the audience doesn't know.

show time!

"Did you ever hear the story of how Harry Houdini broke into a locked safe without opening the door? Well, I'm going to do the exact same trick...without the safe."

STEP 1: Show the audience the second ball and the cup. Make sure they can't see the first ball hidden in the cup! There's a lot more to this trick than that, so get ready.

"I've got this one ball. Let's call him Harry. And since I don't have a safe, this cup will have to do."

STEP 2: Take the cup, and flip it mouth down onto the table. Remember, the cup has the secret ball inside, so flip it quickly and carefully so the ball doesn't fly out. If it does, saying "Hey, look! Harry's twin!" probably won't prevent the audience from knowing you messed up. Hold the ball that's not inside the cup, and show it to the audience.

"I'm going to ask little Harry here to pass through the solid cup and appear underneath. Sometimes Harry gets an attitude and doesn't want to do the trick, so no insults, please. He's very sensitive."

STEP 3: Hold the ball between the first two fingers of your left hand. Make sure the audience can clearly see the ball.

Stick your right fist over the cup with the hidden ball. Put "Harry"—the visible ball—on top of your fist.

"Now, I'll just open my fist and let the ball fall onto the cup."

MAGICIAN'S VIEW

STEP 4: This step is called the *drop vanish*. This is one way of making a ball seem one place when it's really in another. (It's also what happens if you drop the ball, then vanish from the stage.) Loosen the fingers of your right hand so the ball falls into, but NOT through, your fist. Don't let the ball fall onto the cup, but let it rest near your ring finger. Pull your hand away from the cup, revealing that there is no ball on top. You've just done a drop vanish!

"So I'll take this ball and...hey! Where'd it go?"

STEP 5: Keeping the ball palmed in your right hand, quickly lift

the cup with your index finger and thumb, revealing the second ball (which has been hanging out under the cup all along).

"Ah! There he is! Just like Harry Houdini!"

HOMEWORK: There's lots to practice for this trick. The drop vanish can be tricky, so don't be discouraged! You want the motions to be as natural as possible to fool the audience.

Lesson: Force balls to move through cups!

tricky BaLLs

You can bounce a ball. You can throw a ball. And with a hidden ball you can make the audience think you've actually forced one through a cup!

magic must-haves: Magic trunk, magic wand

from your iLLusions kit: Three cups, four balls

Backstage

Listen up! This trick requires more attention than you'd give one of your dad's old stories. The cups are different colors: blue, yellow, and red. Place the blue cup inside the yellow cup, mouth up. Drop one of the fuzzy balls inside the blue cup. Mmmmm. That's good eatin'! Place the red cup, also mouth up, inside the blue cup (on top of the first fuzzy ball). Now, drop the three remaining balls inside the red cup.

show time!

"This magic trick is older than my dad's favorite chair, but it still works today."

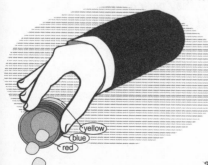

STEP 1: Grab the three cups as one, and pour out the three balls from the red cup onto the magic trunk.

"When it was first done, they used stone balls and bowls. Now it's more modern: I've got these plastic cups…"

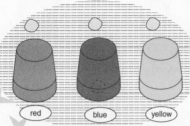

MAGICIAN'S VIEW

red   blue   yellow

STEP 2: Line up the three balls in a row on the trunk. Press on them with your fingers to show the audience that they are soft and fuzzy.

"…and there's nothing more modern than these three fuzzy little balls."

STEP 3: Grab the red cup and turn it mouth down behind the ball on your left. Take the blue cup, and turn it mouth down behind the middle ball. Do this quickly so the ball hidden inside does not fall out and roll away.

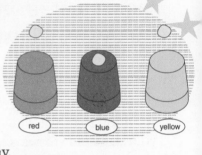

red   blue   yellow

If it does roll away, just yell **"Prison Break!"** and move on to your next trick. Turn over the yellow cup, mouth down, behind the ball on the right.

"Even though they are fuzzy and little…"

Trick Tip: When turning the cups over, hold them around the mouth of the cup. That makes it easier to flip the cups over and keep the hidden ball inside! (And it also keeps the cups from talking to each other.)

STEP 4: Pick up the ball in front of the blue cup, and place it on top of the blue cup. You do remember that the blue cup is the one with the ball hidden underneath it, right?

"…they pack a lot of power."

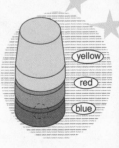

yellow
red
blue

STEP 5: Keeping the ball on top of the blue cup, put the red cup and then the yellow cup mouth down over the blue

cup. Tap the top of the yellow cup with the magic wand.

"When you combine their fuzzy ball power with the power of the magic wand..."

STEP 6: Lift the three cups as one, and turn them mouth up on the magic trunk, revealing one fuzzy ball underneath.

AUDIENCE'S VIEW

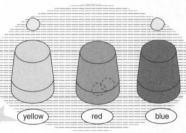

MAGICAN'S VIEW

"...the fuzzy ball will blast its way through one of the cups."

STEP 7: Line up the three balls again. Now, put the blue cup behind the right ball. Take the red cup (the one that still has the hidden ball left over from the previous trick), and place it *over* the middle ball. Then put the yellow cup behind the ball on the left. You should have three cups and two balls showing, and two balls hidden under the red cup. If you don't, then you really have made one of the fuzzy balls disappear and are now Valedictorian Emeritus of Magic! All hail!

"Okay, so that works with one ball, but can I get a second fuzzy ball to go through the cup and join the first one?"

STEP 8: Lift up the ball in front of the yellow cup and place it on top of the red cup.

"Let's see."

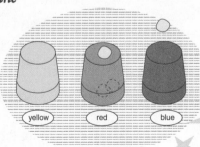

29

STEP 9: Place the blue cup upside down over the red cup. Then place the yellow cup upside down over the blue cup. Tap the top of the upside-down yellow cup twice with the magic wand.

"I may have to use the power of the magic wand twice this time."

AUDIENCE'S VIEW

STEP 10: Lift up the three cups as one, and turn them mouth up. Two balls will appear underneath.

"Let's try this one more time—but let's make it harder."

STEP 11: Take the red cup, and place it to the left. Take the blue cup, and put it over the two balls grouped in the middle. You've now got three balls under the blue cup, but the audience thinks you've got only two. Take the yellow cup, and place it behind the ball remaining—it should be to your right.

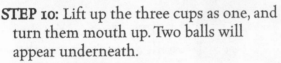

"Can I get the third ball to pass through not one but two cups and join the first two balls?"

STEP 12: Place the red cup upside down over the blue cup. Pick up the right ball, and place it on the bottom of the red cup. Pick up the yellow cup,

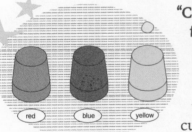

MAGICIAN'S VIEW

36

and turn it upside down over the other two cups. Tap the top of the upside-down yellow cup three times with the magic wand.

"I may have to use three times my magic wand power here."

STEP 13: Lift up the three cups together. Three balls will remain on the magic trunk.

"And sure enough, a fuzzy ball can pass through two cups."

ʜoᴍᴇᴡoʀᴋ: With the ball hidden inside the cup, practice turning it over quickly enough so the ball doesn't fall out.

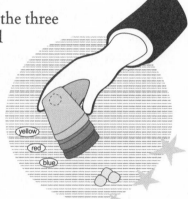

AUDIENCE'S VIEW

CUPS AND BALL BEARINGS

The cups and balls trick is one of the classic tricks by which a true magician's talent is judged. And when we say classic, we mean that this is a really, *really* old trick. The ancient Egyptians (those guys with the mummies and the pyramids) used to do it, and have three little chicks appear under the cups for a grand finale!

The undisputed twentieth century master of the cups and balls was the late Canadian magician Dai Vernon. He was the wise old Merlin of magic. Other magicians would call him "the Professor" and come from all over the world to study the art with him in his castle—the Magic Castle in Hollywood, CA. His secret? "Practice, practice, practice."

the RUBBER BaND JUMP

exercise: Make a rubber band switch fingers!

elastic fantastic

This is an example of a trick that does itself. No, really. If you've got four fingers, you can do this! Just put the rubber bands in the right place, and you can't go wrong. Stretching the rubber band across all four fingernails secretly removes it from two fingers and allows it to "jump" to the other two.

homemade magic: Two rubber bands that are the same size but different colors

backstage

Wash your hands so that your fingers are clean for the performance! Magic doesn't have to be dirty.

show time!

"A rubber band is good for a lot of things. Wrap it around newspapers, shoot it in the air, or use it to tie up packages. But all that stuff's boring. Because I'm a magician, I can make a rubber band jump right through my fingers."

STEP 1: Show the audience that you've got a rubber band wrapped once around the index finger and middle finger of your left hand.

"Like this regular rubber band here. It's on my two fingers."

STEP 2: Curl your fingertips away from the audience, like you're making a fist. Curl them until they are just touching your palm. As you do this, stretch the rubber band out with your right hand.

The rubber band should be around the fingernails of your four left fingers. It should also still be looped around the backs of your left index and middle fingers just below your finger joints. Of course, if you did the **Whopper Chopper** trick

MAGICIAN'S VIEW wrong earlier, forget the part about needing an index finger!

"But not for very long."

STEP 3: Uncurl your fingers— slow, but not too slow; fast, but not too fast. How's that for highly detailed instruction? As you do, the rubber band will automatically jump to your ring and little fingers.

If this didn't work, you might need new fingers. If you can't find any, practice the trick again.

"Cool, huh? Who knew rubber bands were such great escape artists? But let's see just how talented that rubber band is. And for that, I need a second rubber band."

STEP 4: Set up the first rubber band like you did in step 1. Take the second rubber band, and loop it around your little finger, between the tip and the first joint. Twist it once, then loop it over your ring finger, also between the tip and first joint. Twist it once more and loop it over your middle finger, and twist it one last time and loop it over your index finger, both between the tip and the first joint.

"This second rubber band will go over all my fingers to try to stop my first rubber band from jumping."

STEP 5: Repeat step 2 exactly. "Or will it?"

STEP 6: Uncurl your fingers. The rubber band jumps to your other fingers, just like it did before!

"Score: Rubber bands 2, Magician 0. I guess when a rubber band wants to jump, there's nothing you can do to stop it."

HOMEWORK: In front of a mirror, practice stretching the rubber band over your curled fingers.

THE SILK MASTER

The first magician to perform with silk handkerchiefs was Bautier de Kolta from Lyon, France. Silk was a natural material for him to use because in the 1880s, Lyon was the silk capital of Europe. His *Cocoon Illusion* featured a woman dressed in a silk butterfly costume bursting out of an apparently empty silk cocoon. De Kolta never revealed the secret to this illusion, but we can only guess that it used some pretty keen optical effects.

project: Make all three cups face mouth up in three moves.

sequence of events

The trick is to put the cups in the proper sequence before you start flipping. Actually, the sequence is the second most important thing. The most important is to make certain there's no water in the cups; otherwise, you're in for a flood!

magic must-haves: Magic trunk

from your illusions kit: Three cups

backstage

Nothing to do here, so get out there and dazzle 'em!

show time!

"The thing I love most about homework is that it gives me plenty of opportunity to think of other things to do rather than homework. In fact, just last night, rather than study history, I came up with a cool trick."

STEP 1: Take the three cups, and place them on the magic trunk. The outside cups should be mouth down, and the middle cup should be mouth up. The cups must be in this sequence for the trick to work.

"I've got these three cups here. Watch me as I flip them from upside down to right side up, or from right side up to upside down. I have to flip two cups in each turn and I've got to get all three cups to be right side up in exactly three turns. Not more than three turns, not less than three turns. Exactly three. Why? Hey, it's my trick. I can make up any rules I want. Watch closely!"

End of turn 1

End of turn 2

End of turn 3

STEP 2: Flip over the center and right cups (turn 1). Now flip over the two outside cups (turn 2). Finally, flip over the center and right cup one last time (turn 3). *Voilà!* All three cups should be mouth up.

STEP 3: Now, set up the cups again, but this time, flip the cups over so the two outer cups are mouth up and the center cup is mouth down. Then ask for a volunteer.

"Hey, that was easy, right? So easy, I bet you think you can do what I did. Come on up and try it. Here are the rules again: You must flip two cups during each turn. You've got exactly three turns, and you can't take any more or any fewer. After you've taken all three turns, all three cups have got to be right side up."

> **Trick Tip:** If you flip the cups quickly, no one will notice the difference in the way you set up the cups in step 1 and step 3.

STEP 4: Guess what? With the cups set up this way, your volunteer won't be able to get all three cups right side up in three turns, no matter what he tries!
"Hey, that's strange. I wonder why it didn't work for you. They must not make cups the way they used to."

HOMEWORK: Practice memorizing how to place the cups and the order in which you flip 'em.

MIRROR, MIRROR

Magicians not only use mirrors to practice with but also to fool people. In 1913, the English magicians Maskelyne and Devant had their own London theater called Egyptian Hall, where they made an image of miniature people appear inside a crystal. Creating the tiny people is believed to have been done with special mirrors.

pROjeCt: Link two paper clips together with a dollar bill.

LiNkaGe

If you think of paper clips as just boring school supplies, think again. Here's a cool trick that links them together, using only a dollar bill. The folds of the dollar automatically push apart the sides of the paper clips, then link them together as you pull at the ends of the bill.

maGic must-Haves: Magic trunk

HomemaDe maGic: Two big paper clips, a dollar bill, a rubber band

BackstaGe

Relax. You've got almost nothing hard to do here—just set the paper clips, the dollar, and the rubber band on your magic trunk. (If you want to make this trick really challenging—and profitable—try borrowing the dollar from someone in the audience and then keeping it when the trick is over (just kidding)!)

sHoW time!

"I love going down to the magic store and learning all the new tricks. They have this really cool one called the Chinese Linking Rings where you can hook solid rings together to make a chain. I wanted to get it but I'd spent all my money on video games and only had this dollar left over."

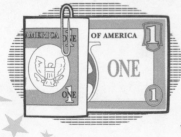

STEP 1: Take the dollar and fold one third of it over onto itself. Slide a paper clip onto the fold.

"But I came up with my own version of that trick, using my leftover dollar."

STEP 2: Take the remaining third of the dollar, and fold it back in the opposite way of the previous fold. Clip it to the middle third of the dollar.

"I just fold the dollar like this and clip it with these regular paper clips. And when I pull the dollar apart..."

STEP 3: Quickly pull the ends of the dollar bill apart. The paper clips will fly into the air. Feel free to duck as they shoot out! When they land, they'll be hooked together.

"Cool, huh? But I didn't want paper clips flying all over the house. Paper clips are shockingly expensive, and I can't afford to lose any. So I came up with a variation."

STEP 4: Loop a rubber band once around the width of the bill. Now, fold the bill, and clip it exactly as you did in steps 1 and 2. Make sure the rubber band ends up in the middle of the folds. Be certain that it fits comfortably around the bill, but not so tight that the bill crinkles. Crinkled bills make for bad magic tricks and unhappy ducks.

Trick Tip: This trick works best with a crisp, new dollar bill.

"I added a rubber band."

STEP 5: Now, pull the ends of the bill apart quickly. The paper clips are linked together and attached to the rubber band!

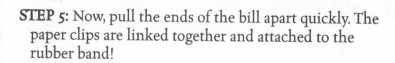

"Now the paper clips are still linked together, but they're also attached to the rubber band! So it's easy for me to keep track of those paper clips."

HOMEWORK: Practice pulling apart the ends of the bill—you don't want to go too slow or too fast.

TRICK LINKING

Paper Clipped is very similar to the famous *Chinese Linking Rings*. No one knows when it was first performed in China, but the first performance in Europe was by a nineteenth-century Frenchman known only as Philippe. Many methods have been used to link and unlink what appear to be solid rings of steel. One simple method is to simply switch two unlinked rings for two linked ones when the audience is momentarily distracted.

STRiNG-a-LONG

#II

Lesson: Cut string into two pieces, and magically restore it to one piece!

it's Not a kNot

The secret to this string trick is not the string, it's the knot. Got it? By tying the knot exactly as shown and cutting at the right place, you create a small piece of string that's separate from the longer piece. That small piece is really what you're cutting off, even though it looks like you've cut the string in half.

Homemade magic:

About 2 feet of rope or clothesline, a pair of scissors

> **Trick Tip:** Softer is always better. Use a piece of rope or clothesline that feels soft. The softer it feels, the easier it is to handle while performing the trick!

Backstage

If you've got the rope and the scissors, you're good to go!

Show time!

"I love rope because it makes for a good magic trick."

STEP 1: Hold the rope in front of the audience, and pull on the ends. Let them see that it's all one piece. Then lay the rope across the open palm of your left hand. (You laughed earlier, but we bet you're glad now that the rope is soft!)

"I take this simple piece of rope..."

STEP 2: With your right hand, bring up one end of the rope, and drape it over the top of the middle of the rope. Loop it around, right over left, to make a knot. But don't pull the knot too tight! Leave a loop in the rope.

"...and I tie a knot in it, like this...."

STEP 3: Next, tie the front end of the rope around the back end of the rope, left over right. Pull the knot tight.

"Now, we're ready for the cutting."

STEP 4: With your left hand holding the rope, pick up the scissors, and with one snip, cut through the short end that's hanging down and the loop that's next to it. Don't worry, we never liked this loop anyway—it deserves to be cut out of the act. A piece of the short end should fly off as you snip. (The short end is the end that sticks out of the knot.)

"Now I've cut the rope."

STEP 5: Put the scissors down. Stretch out the rope between your hands so that it's straight, but don't pull it tight yet. It should look like you've got a rope knot in the center of the rope. (It's really just a short piece of rope!)

"But I've got this annoying knot in the center. I'd better get rid of it."

STEP 6: Pull sharply on the rope with both hands. The little piece of rope will fly off, and the knot will disappear! The rope is now in one piece again!

"And that's why I love a good rope trick!"

HOMEWORK: Practice making the knot until you can do it without thinking about it.

Trick Tip: Sooner or later, you'll have snipped through enough rope that you'll need a new piece. Buy a bunch of rope so that you'll always have some on hand for practice. No one ever said magic was cheap!

THE MAGIC OF ROPE

Magicians having been doing magic with rope and string for more than four hundred years. Probably the one trick that everyone knows is the *Hindu Rope Trick* or *Indian Rope Trick*. This dates back to somewhere between 618–906 C.E. In one version, a mystic throws a rope into the air where it remains rigid. A boy climbs to the top of the rope and then vanishes. Although only a few people claim to have ever seen this trick, that hasn't stopped magicians from trying to figure out the secret. Most American magicians believe that the *Hindu Rope Trick* is a legend and has never actually been performed.

PENNILESS

#12

assignment: Make a penny pass through someone's hand!

penny-wise

Who would have thought that counting pennies would make a terrific sleight-of-hand trick? We did. And you will, too, once you make some poor audience member think you've put seven pennies in his hand. But the reality is you've only given him six. The seventh penny remains hidden in your hand.

magic must-haves: Magic trunk

homemade magic: Seven pennies

extras: One volunteer who doesn't know the trick

backstage

An easy trick with no backstage shenanigans. Just relax and double count your pennies so you're sure to start with all seven. (And if you have trouble counting all the way up to seven, you should consider enrolling in Math University instead.)

show time!

"To ordinary humans, pennies are totally boring. But to magicians like me—they're totally boring, too! I still keep 'em, though, because I can still use them for magic. One thing I can do with pennies is make them pass through human skin."

STEP 1: Place the seven pennies on the magic trunk. Find a volunteer, and ask her to step right up.

"I've got seven pennies here, and I want you to pick them

up off the trunk and then drop them in my hand one at a time. Count them out loud as you do it, okay? You do know how to count to seven, right?"

STEP 2: If she can't, oh, brother! Get a new volunteer! Hold out your right hand, and let her count out the pennies. When she's finished, pick up one penny with your left hand.

"Now don't be scared, but I can make this penny pass through your hand."

STEP 3: Still holding that penny in your left hand, place (don't drop!) the other six pennies, one at a time, from your right hand to the right hand of your volunteer, and count them as you do it. Clink the pennies against each other as you place them. (The clinking sound helps reinforce the count in everyone's mind.)

Trick Tip: This is a trick that depends on sound to reinforce the counting. Make sure you clink the coins as you count! You can try making the clink noise with your tongue against your teeth, but that just looks silly.

"One, two, three, four, five..."

STEP 4: On the sixth penny, clink it against the others, say "six" out loud, but keep it in your fingers. Use your thumb to quickly slide it and hide it between your index finger and your middle finger.

"...six..."

STEP 5: Reach over with your left hand and place the seventh penny (which you've been keeping in your left hand) on top of the other five pennies in your volunteer's right hand.

"...and seven. All seven pennies are in your hand."

STEP 6: Put your right hand (the one holding and hiding the sixth penny) under the volunteer's hand (the one holding the six pennies), and hold it so that your palm is under the back of her hand.

"Now I'm going to make that penny pass through your very skin, right through the bone, past the blood vessels, the icky tissue, and the gross muscles."

STEP 7: Tap the top of her hand with your left hand.

"And away it goes!"

STEP 8: Pull out your hand from underneath hers. Open it up to reveal that you have one of the pennies.

"Now open your hand, and show me what you've got. And count them out loud if you don't mind."

STEP 9: Your volunteer will count out six pennies! But only if you've picked a volunteer who can count that high.

"And you said you knew how to count to seven..."

HOMEWORK: Practice hiding the sixth penny as you clink it against the others in step 4.

MAGIC OF THE DEAD

Boo! Magicians aren't the only ones to cause strange things to happen. In the late nineteenth century, many mediums claimed to be in contact with the spirit world. The Fox sisters, who were six and eight years old and came from Hydesville, New York, claimed to communicate with ghosts. People came from hundreds of miles away to hear the spirits "knock" or "tap" a response to a given question. Thirty years later, Margaret Fox confessed the secret source of those rapping noises: The girls had been secretly cracking their finger and toe knuckles!

saw the STRAW #13

Lesson: Cut a drinking straw in half without cutting the string inside!

straw sawing

Straws are great for slurping up your favorite drink, but you can also use them for magic when you're done. Using a secret slit in the straw, a pair of scissors can cut through the straw and above the string. The straw gets snipped in two pieces, and the string remains uncut!

magic must-haves: Magic trunk

Homemade magic:

A piece of string, a drinking straw, a small pair of scissors, one million dollars (Okay, you don't really need a million dollars to do this trick, but it sure would be cool, right?)

> **Trick Tip:** Your straw can be any color except clear. A clear straw reveals the slit!

Backstage

Once again, you're making your own gimmick. Cut the piece of string so that it's about 4 inches longer than the straw. Cut a small slit lengthwise, about an inch each way from the center of the straw. If you're doing the math, that makes the total slit about 2 inches long. Put the piece of string and the straw on the magic trunk.

show time!

"One of magic's oldest tricks is sawing a woman in half. A lovely lady is placed in a box and cut into two pieces, but she comes out in one piece. Well, none of my friends wanted to be cut in two, but not to worry, I can use a substitute."

STEP 1: Pick up the piece of string from the magic trunk.

"Here is my beautiful substitute lady. She's a little on the boring side, but hey, you can't have everything."

STEP 2: Pick up the straw with your other hand, and hold it with the slit facing you so that the audience can't see it.

"And here is the box."

STEP 3: Thread the string through the straw so that it dangles evenly out of both ends.

"Now, I'll place my beautiful substitute lady inside the box. And now for the sawing in half part!"

STEP 4: Bend the straw in half. Pick up the scissors, and insert the point through the slit of the straw but above the string. Keep your palm wrapped around the straw to cover the string when it pops out from the slit and…cut! You're cutting the straw all the way through.

"Ouch. That's got to hurt…except for one thing…"

STEP 5: Slide apart the two pieces of the straw— the string is uncut!

"My lady is just as beautiful as she was at the beginning!"

HOMEWORK: Practice bending the straw, hiding the string so it doesn't stick out of the straw slit, and cutting the straw.

I SAW HALF A WOMAN

In 1920, the English magician P. T. Selbit invented the world's most popular trick, sawing a woman in half. It was an immediate sensation. In Selbit's original version, the woman stepped into a long box and had her feet and head strapped down. When the lid was closed and she was completely out of view, she would secretly slip her feet out of the straps and curl up in a ball as the saw cut the box into two separate halves. Over the years many improvements have been made with this illusion. The most important is keeping the woman's head and feet in full view at all times. Today in Las Vegas, a number of magicians perform a version of this illusion in which there is no box. The magician is strapped to a table, and the audience can see a huge buzz saw cut right through the magician's middle, leaving him unharmed!

exercise: Pass two cards through the deck and into your hand!

passing cards

Want to fool with the audience and totally play with their heads? Then this simple sleight-of-hand trick is for you. The seven and eight of clubs look similar to the seven and eight of spades—similar enough to fool the audience! Check 'em out! Did it fool you, too? If you said yes, you should probably move on to the next trick.

magic must-haves: Magic trunk

Homemade magic: A deck of normal playing cards

backstage

Place the eight of clubs on the top of the deck and the seven of spades on the bottom. (Or, if you're feeling rebellious, put the eight of clubs on the bottom of the deck and the seven of spades on the top!)

faceup

Remove the eight of spades and the seven of clubs, and set them facedown on the magic trunk. Take the rest of the deck, and place it facedown, away from the two cards.

show time!

"Magician's hands and playing cards go together like cheese and a burger. They're made for each other."

facedown

STEP 1: Hold up the eight of spades and the seven of clubs so the audience can see them.

"I've got two cards here, a black seven and a black eight."

STEP 2: Slide them facedown into the middle of the deck.

"And I've hidden the seven and eight in the middle of a deck of normal playing cards."

STEP 3: Hold the deck with your fingers on the bottom and your thumb on the top. Flick your wrist, and squeeze the rest of the deck from your hand while simultaneously pressing your thumb and fingers together. Be careful! If you do this too hard, you'll throw the deck at the audience. If that happens, at least aim the deck at someone you don't like.

"But because I'm a magician, I can pull those two cards through the deck."

STEP 4: Now you've got only two cards in your hand—the card that was on top of the deck and the card that was on the bottom. Show the two cards to the audience. This is where the fooling part comes in. It's the eight of clubs and the seven of spades, but everyone will be too busy wondering why you threw the deck at that guy in the second row to notice the switch. And even if you don't throw the deck at that guy in the second row, they still won't notice the switch.

Trick Tip: Don't identify the suits of the cards by name—only by number and color; let the audience think for themselves!

HOMEWORK: Practice dropping the deck while keeping the top and bottom card squeezed between your fingers. Be careful when the cards splat everywhere!

TRICK GLOVES?

The magician known as Cardini had his own style. He wore a top hat and a monocle and plucked cards out of thin air with his white-gloved hands. He was born in 1894 in a Welsh fishing village and performed all over the world, including Chicago's famous Palmer House Hotel in the 1920s. How did he make the cards appear? Cardini never published the secret, but some people suspect it was the gloves. What do you think?

tHe PaiNLeSS BALLOON #15

assiGNMENt: Don't pop a balloon with a pin!

BaLLOON-a-trick

Balloons always pop when stuck with a pin—but you've gimmicked one of your balloons! The clear tape acts as a "bandage" that prevents the balloon from popping.

MaGiC MuSt-HaVeS:

Magic trunk

HomeMaDe MaGiC:

Two pieces of clear tape, two balloons, one pin

BaCKStaGe

Take a deep breath—this trick requires some big exhaling. Blow up two balloons so that they are approximately the same size. Place two pieces of clear tape in an X shape on one of them, but leave the other tapeless. Place the two balloons on the magic trunk in front of you. *Don't let the audience see the tape!*

sHow time!

"The dog chases the cat, big fish eat little fish, and pins love to pop balloons."

STEP 1: Hold up the tapeless balloon with one hand and the pin with the other. Impersonate the balloon as you wave it around, trying to keep it away from the pin.

"'No, please, Mr. Pin, please don't stick me! Nooooo!' But the balloon can't get away, and so it gets popped."

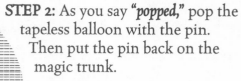

STEP 2: As you say **"popped,"** pop the tapeless balloon with the pin. Then put the pin back on the magic trunk.

"But suppose I could hypnotize a balloon, make it think it's big and strong and that a pin can't hurt it?"

STEP 3: Stare intensely at the taped balloon. Wave your hand around it, act like you're hypnotizing it. Talk to the balloon in a calm, reassuring voice.

"You are a strong balloon. You are a tough balloon. You have a skin of steel. No pin can harm you."

STEP 4: Stop staring at the balloon, and pick up the pin.

"The balloon is now completely hypnotized and totally under my spell. It will not let itself be popped."

STEP 5: Stick the pin through the center of the X of tape. The balloon won't pop!

"And there you have it—the toughest balloon in the world, thanks to the magic of hypnosis!"

STEP 6: Now, turn to someone in the audience and say how you want to try it on him. Hold up the pin, look at him, and say, *"You are a strong balloon. You are a tough balloon..."* This is usually where they run out of the room screaming.

> **Trick Tip:** You're going to pop a lot of balloons as you learn and perform this trick. Buy a big bag of them!

> **Trick Tip #2:** Be careful with the taped balloon—it might pop when you pull the pin out (or even while the pin's still in the balloon)! If it does, just say, "I guess the hypnosis wore off. That's one strong-willed balloon!"

HOMEWORK: Try different-size pieces of tape on the balloon.

TWIST AND TURN

Magicians have had a thing for sticking pins and swords and other sharp objects into people and balloons for hundreds of years. A classic illusion performed in India is the *Basket Trick*. A boy gets inside a basket that is then run through with many swords. The swords are then removed and the boy leaps out unharmed. The secret lies in the boy's ability to dodge each sword as it is thrust through the basket. And you thought dodgeball was tough!

PASSiNG GLaSS #16

project: Smack a glass through a table!

GLass passiNG

If you want a trick that really makes the audience jump, this is it. It's great sleight-of-hand magic that catches the audience completely by surprise. A paper "mold" of a drinking glass makes the audience think the glass is still on the table. After you smash the paper, they're shocked when you pull out the real glass from under the table!

maGic must-Haves: Magic wand

Homemade maGic: Plastic drinking glass, a sheet of newspaper, a quarter

Backstage

For this trick to work, you have to sit at a table. That's it. You. Table. Sit.

SHow time!

"I've got a normal drinking glass, a sheet of newspaper, and my lucky quarter."

STEP 1: Hold up the drinking glass, and set it on the table, upside down.

"Now, I'm going to make this quarter go right through the table! But first, I've gotta get the glass ready."

STEP 2: Cover the drinking glass with the newspaper, and mold it with your hand until it's in the shape of the glass. The newspaper should completely cover the glass. Place the quarter on the table, about a foot from the edge.

"First I cover the glass..."

STEP 3: Place the covered glass over the coin. Tap the top of the glass three times.

"Now, I place the covered glass over my quarter for just a quick second...and the quarter should be..."

STEP 4: Lift up the glass. Surprise! The coin is still there. Look disappointed, then act like you just remembered something.

"Shoot! I must have...of course! I forgot the magic wand!"

STEP 5: Put the covered glass back over the quarter. Tap the top three times with the magic wand.

"Abracadabra! And the quarter is..."

STEP 6: Lift up the covered glass. The quarter is still there. Only now when you remove the glass, slide it over the top of the table toward you. Sweep it off the edge and loosen your grip on the glass. The glass falls into your lap while you hold the newspaper. The newspaper should keep the same shape, as if the glass was still there.

"All right, let's try this one more time."

STEP 7: Place the paper on top of the quarter again. *WHAM!* Quickly slam your right hand on top of the paper like you just crushed the glass! As you slam, reach under the table with your left hand. As you pull

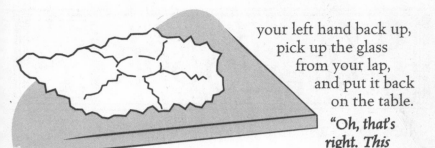

your left hand back up, pick up the glass from your lap, and put it back on the table.

"Oh, that's right. *This is a trick that makes the glass go through the table! I'll save the coin for next time.*"

Trick Tip: If the newspaper's not taking the shape of the glass, try this trick with aluminum foil—it's easier to mold and holds its shape a lot better. And it's great for keeping sandwiches fresh, too!

HOMEWORK: Work on your sliding-glass technique—practice sliding the glass off the table and into your lap as you hold onto the newspaper mold.

A HATFUL OF GLASS

Max Malini was a master of tricks with drinking glasses. Born in Ostrov, Poland, in 1873, he grew up in the Bowery in New York City and lived in Chicago when not performing for kings, queens, and presidents. He'd place a coin on a restaurant table and cover it with his hat. "Heads or tails?" he'd ask. After he had his answer, he'd lift his hat to reveal a full glass of liquid. How did he do it? Misdirection. Malini was an expert at it!

THE PAPER DOOR #17

LESSON: Walk through a piece of paper!

WALK THROUGH PAPER

If you're old enough to hold a pair of scissors, you can make a door out of a piece of paper. This is a goofy trick, but it's really fun. By cutting a piece of paper in just the right places, you create a giant square strip that's big enough to walk through.

HOMEMADE MAGIC: A piece of letter-size paper, scissors

SHOW TIME!

"Paper has a lot of magic properties, but it takes a real magician to be able to bring them out."

STEP 1: Hold up the piece of paper so that the audience can see that there's nothing tricky about it. Let them touch it or hold it themselves if you want.

"This piece of paper, for example, is really a door that I can walk right through."

STEP 2: Take the paper and fold it in half, lengthwise.

"The secret to walking through a piece of paper is finding the hidden door. The guy who invented paper was pretty tricky."

STEP 3: With the scissors, cut from the fold almost to the edge, several times. Each cut should be about 2 inches from the previous cut.

"But if you know what you're doing and cut along the secret passageway ..."

STEP 4: Turn the paper around so that it's facing the opposite direction. Now cut between the slits you've made, but start from the edge this time, and cut almost to the fold. Don't cut past the fold!

"...and then you cut some more..."

STEP 5: Turn the paper around again so that it's back in the position you started in step 2. Except for the first and last folds, cut through the top of each of the other folds.

"...very quickly, you can find the door..."

STEP 6: Now open up the paper, and show the hole to the audience.

"...and walk right through it!"

Trick Tip: You can experiment with different-colored paper or by adjusting the length of your cuts to make the hole different sizes.

HOMEWORK: Practice cutting with the scissors so you can do it smoothly—don't cut yourself, and don't cut the paper in the wrong place!

THICK AS A BRICK

On July 13, 1914, Harry Houdini had workers build a solid brick wall on the stage of the New York Hippodrome. The wall was surrounded by a group of volunteers. Small screens were placed on both sides of the wall. Houdini went behind one screen and then reappeared behind the other, having apparently walked through the brick wall. It is believed that he went through trapdoors on either side of the walls; however, Houdini covered the floor with a solid carpet to eliminate this possibility. So the question remains: How did he really do it?

Napkin magic #18

project: Tie two napkins together, and then pull them apart!

end over end

This is not a naughty trick, it's a knotty trick—while it looks like you're tying two napkins together, you're really not. The "knot" doesn't exist! You might say it's a "not knot."

Homemade magic: Two cloth napkins, preferably the same color

> **Trick Tip:** While you're practicing this trick, feel free to use napkins that are different colors—that'll help you understand how the "knot" works.

backstage

Make sure the napkins are clean—you might want to do this trick before dinner, just to be sure!

show time!

"I went to a fancy restaurant with my parents and some friends of theirs. All they did was talk about stuff I wasn't interested in. It was pretty boring."

STEP 1: This is another one of those "pay attention closely" tricks, so pay attention closely. Roll up the two napkins, and lay them down, one on top of the other, so they look like a "+" sign. The horizontal napkin should be on top.

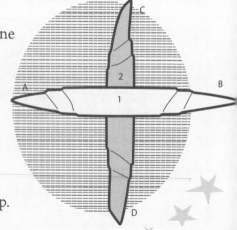

"Before dinner, I was so bored, I decided to do a magic trick and tell the story of two friends of mine, Tim and Louise. To illustrate my story, I used two napkins."

STEP 2: Let's call the horizontal napkin that's on top napkin #1, and the vertical napkin that's on the bottom napkin #2. Take napkin #1, and fold the right end (B in the picture) under napkin #2. It should come out between the left end of napkin #1 (A) and the top end of napkin #2 (C).

"They met in history class and really connected. Pretty soon they were going everywhere together."

STEP 3: Now, take the left end of napkin #1 (A) and wrap it underneath napkin #2. The ends of napkin #1 should be pointing in opposite directions.

"They'd go to the mall."

STEP 4: Take the top end of napkin #2 (C) and wrap it once over napkin #1.

"They'd go to the movies."

STEP 5: Take the bottom end of napkin #2 (D), and wrap it once over the top of napkin #1. This is the really tricky part, so read carefully! When you do this step, you are not really twisting napkin #2 over napkin #1. You have to quickly and carefully lift the knot with your left hand and tuck napkin #2 behind the knot but over the right end of napkin #1 (B).

"They'd sit together at lunch."

STEP 6: If you've done this correctly, it should look a little bit like a "+" sign with a knot in the center. If it looks right, take the tips of napkin #2 (C & D) and bring them to your right and the tips of napkin #1 (A & B) to your left.

"But soon they had a big fight and they broke up."

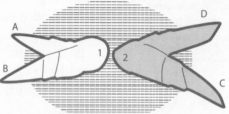

STEP 7: Slowly pull the napkins apart, pulling napkin #2 to your right and napkin #1 to your left. The "knot" dissolves as they separate.

"Now they're not speaking to each other at all."

HOMEWORK: Creating the "knot" in step 5 is the key to the whole trick. Study the pictures, and practicing "tying" it again and again.

DINNERTIME MAGIC

Miracles with ordinary dinner table objects were the specialty of Albert Goshman. In the 1950s, Goshman arrived at the Magic Castle in Hollywood, California, where for the next thirty years he performed his trademark *Saltshaker and Half-Dollar* routine. Every time a spectator picked up a salt shaker there was a half-dollar underneath it. How did he do it? You got it: Misdirection! While he distracted the spectator with his jokes and blue eyes, he picked up the salt shaker and stuck the coin under it.

assignment: Push a magic wand through someone's belly button.

How deep is a BeLLy ButtoN?

This is an optical illusion. Your magic wand has one end that slides back and forth. By pushing on one end as you pull back on the other, it creates the illusion that the wand is piercing your volunteer's belly button.

Homemade magic: Cardboard tube from a dry cleaner's hanger or flat piece of thin cardboard (like the kind you find inside a new shirt), black electrical tape or duct tape, two 2-inch by 3-inch strips of white paper, glue

extras: A volunteer who's in on the trick!

Backstage

For this trick to work you need to create a special magic wand. Get a hanger from the dry cleaner that is used to hang pants—the kind that's got a wire hook and a cardboard tube at the bottom. Take the cardboard tube from the hanger; that's the core of your wand. If you don't have this kind of a hanger, get a thin piece of cardboard (like the kind you find inside a new shirt), roll it into a long tube, and glue it closed. Cover the tube with the black electrical tape or duct tape.

The magic wand needs a white end, and you're going to make two. Take one strip of paper, and roll it around one end of the wand, and glue it in place. Take

the second strip of paper, and roll it loosely around the other end so that it can slide easily along your wand. Glue the ends of this strip together. When you're ready to begin the trick, move the sliding tip all the way to the non-sliding end of the wand, so that it covers the non-sliding tip.

SHOW time!

"This is a special trick, and I'm going to need someone from the audience to help me."

STEP 1: Look around the audience like you're thinking of whom to call on. Point to your secret volunteer.

"This is all about the belly button. Everyone's got one. And a lot of people play with them, sticking their finger in to see just how far it goes."

STEP 2: Press your finger into your belly button.

"As a magician, that's something I already know. I'll show you."

STEP 3: Grab the nonsliding end of the wand with your left hand, so that it covers that end of the wand. Press it against your volunteer's stomach. Then grab the sliding end of the wand with your right hand.

"I'll use my magic wand as my measuring stick."

STEP 4: With your right hand, push the sliding tip toward your volunteer, just a little bit.

"First, I've got to get through the little layer of protective skin…"

"…past all the dirt and lint in there…"

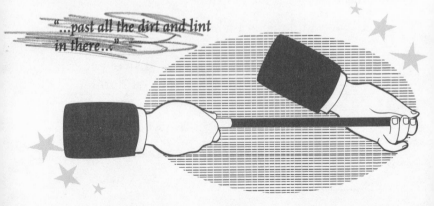

STEP 5: Keep pushing the sliding end toward your volunteer with your right hand. The rest of the wand should be covered by your right arm. This blocks the audience from seeing the whole wand. Act like you're pushing really hard. Make a face like you're struggling. It should look like the wand is going into your volunteer's belly!

"The trick is to get it past the kidneys and the liver and not do any damage to the body."

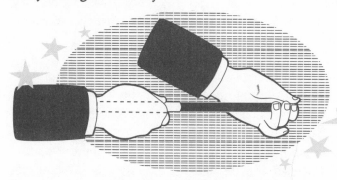

STEP 6: Stop about five inches down the wand. Pause and look at the audience so they can see that the wand has gone through the belly button.

"I think that's as far as it'll go."

STEP 7: Look at your volunteer. Now slowly slide your right hand back toward you, and begin moving the sliding tube toward the end of the wand. Act like it's not easy—not as difficult as you made it seem earlier, but still hard to pull out.

"But don't worry, I won't leave it in there."

STEP 8: Finish pulling the sliding tube to the end of the wand, and then show the wand to the audience. Be sure you cover the "tipless" end of the wand with your hand!

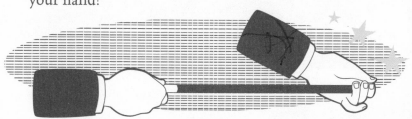

"Well, I guess it can go pretty far. My friend here must really have a deep belly button."

HOMEWORK: In front of a mirror, use your right arm to block the wand so that it can't be seen by the audience.

AIR MAGIC

Everyone loves money, especially magic tricks with money. T. Nelson Downs, who was known as "The King of Koins," made a trick, *The Miser's Dream,* famous. In it he seemed to pluck coins out of the air! Downs was born in Iowa in 1876 and became a great vaudeville star in both England and America because of his amazing ability to manipulate coins. Of course, Downs couldn't *really* grab money from the air. He revealed his secrets in a book called *Modern Coin Magic* published in 1900. However, the sleight-of-hand steps were so difficult that few magicians could duplicate his coin tricks. But he did reveal that he could keep a coin from an audience's view by secretly rotating it from the front to the back of his hand.

the SQUISHY PENCIL #20

PROJECT: Push a pencil through a quarter!

PENCIL LEADER

Are you strong enough to push a pencil through a
solid coin (without using the Three-hole Coin Box)?
You can with this classic misdirection illusion! By
hiding the pencil behind your ear and slamming your
hands together, you can make it seem like your pencil
has gone right through a quarter.

HOMEMADE MAGIC: One quarter, one pencil

BACKSTAGE

The seating arrangements are important for this trick,
so make sure the audience is standing off to your left
before you start. And put any troublemakers way in
the back. The less they see, the better!

SHOW TIME!

"Quarters aren't really as tough as they think they are."

STEP 1: Hold the coin in your
left palm and the pencil in
your right.

*"You might think that's just
bold talk, but I can prove it."*

STEP 2:
Squint
with
one eye,
and take
careful aim. No,
not at the audience! At the
quarter! Raise the pencil to
the right side of your head by
your ear.

"I'm going to push this pencil through this quarter. All I have to do is strike the quarter right in the center. Right through George Washington's nose. Like this!"

STEP 3: Bring the pencil down quickly, and let the tip of the pencil hit the quarter. Do this two more times so that the audience is paying close attention to your quarter.

"One...two..."

STEP 4: On the third time, raise the pencil to the right side of your head, and secretly slip it behind your right ear. Sure, you look a little silly, but who cares? It's magic! See? This is why the audience had to be on your left! They shouldn't see the pencil.

"Three!"

STEP 5: With the pencil snug in its hiding place, on the count of three quickly slam your right hand down to your left hand, open palm striking open palm.

"Wow! I hit the quarter so hard..."

STEP 6: Open up your hands, and show them to the audience. The pencil is gone!

"...that the pencil has vanished!"

HOMEWORK: Practice turning your body slightly away from the mirror (your audience) so even you can't see the pencil when you hide it behind your ear.

> **Trick Tip:** You can also do this trick with a pen or cotton swab—anything that you can hide behind your ear! Heck, even your younger brother will work if your ear is big enough.

A KISS IS JUST A KISS

Harry Houdini, the world's greatest escape artist, was born in Budapest, Hungary, and moved to Appleton, Wisconsin, in 1874. He boasted that no prison could hold him, and he proved this too many times to count. Wearing only a pair of shorts—to demonstrate he had nothing to hide—Houdini would let himself be locked in a cell, only to step out minutes later. How did he do it? The love of a good woman! Just before he went to jail, his wife would give him a kiss and pass a pick from her mouth to his.

CONCLUSION

Congratulations! You've pushed yourself through Illusions, your second course at good ol' Magic U!

You've forced a pencil through a quarter, tied a knot that wasn't there, and smacked a drinking glass through your dining room table—without making your mom mad. Your fingers are probably tired (and so, probably, are the quarters, the rope, and the glasses), but that might be an illusion, too! Take a quick break, and soak up the warm glow of your accomplishments. You might as well: There's no graduation ceremony yet—we've made your diploma disappear!

Do you know what's real and what's an illusion? If you still have trouble with that simple question, then you have to spend more time practicing. The idea is for you to know the answer and to keep your friends, neighbors, and relatives guessing and demanding to know the secrets that you keep to yourself.

Don't disappear! We'll be back next month with your third course: More tricks and trickery, more lessons, more practice, and, of course, more magic! Up next? Mentalism.

about magician
jeff fredriksen

ABOUT JEFF FREDRIKSEN, ALSO KNOWN AS JEFFERY THE GREAT

To do great magic, you need more than a good teacher, you need a great one. Our guest professor for this month's Illusions Course at Magic University isn't just a great teacher and a great magician, he's "Jeffery the Great!"

Jeffery didn't start out with the middle name "the" and the last name "Great." He started out as Jeff Fredriksen. But then the magic bug bit him when he was just about ten years old. That's when he got a magic kit for Christmas. That was all it took!

After that, he discovered a magic shop in his hometown of Chicago, Illinois. His life would never be the same. Each week he spent his allowance on magic tricks, books, and accessories. Then he would practice each trick over and over, learning the art of magic and perfecting his skills. It wasn't too long before he was performing for his family, neighborhood friends, and classmates.

When he was twenty-one years old, his magic hobby became a career. If you live near Chicago, you might see him entertaining at schools, libraries, park districts, and all kinds of private parties.

But the magic never stops! Jeff also wrote and starred in his own local cable show, *It's All Magic*. And with a name like "Jeffery the Great," you can bet he's doing even more: He'll soon star in a big production that mixes magic and the circus. This giant spectacular will showcase his talents in magic as well as tumbling, juggling, and large illusions—big versions of the tricks in this book!

Most of all, Jeff loves magic and hopes you have the same dream he does: Making people smile with wonder and amazement as they try to figure out your magic!

WHAT'S NEW WITH tom mason AND DAN DANKO

TOM MASON

Didn't you learn enough about us last month? Just in case you didn't, here's what's new: Tom just finished writing a brand-new internet project called *Xtreme 'Bot Smackdown!*

DAN DANKO

Is there more to learn about Dan Danko? Possibly. But in the meantime, he's busy writing his latest unsold screenplay for a famous actress who doesn't return his phone calls.